D0576589

Getting To Know...

Nature's Children

LEOPARDS

Sheila Dalton

SCHOLASTIC INC.

New York Toronto London Auckland Sydney
Mexico City New Delhi Hong Kong Buenos Aires

Facts in Brief

Classification of the Leopard

    Class: *Mammalia* (mammals)

    Order: *Carnivora* (meat-eaters)

    Family: *Felidae* (cat family)

    Genus: *Panthera*

    Species: *Panthera pardus* (leopard)

World distribution. Southern Africa, Southern Asia; scattered populations in northern Africa, Arabia, the Far East.

Habitat. Can live in almost any habitat as long as there is enough food and water and a certain amount of cover from which to hunt.

Distinctive physical characteristics. Most have black spots arranged in rosettes on a tawny background. Whiskers are very developed for hunting at night; long, thick tail.

Habits. Basically solitary. Hunts mainly at night.

Diet. Small animals and the young of larger species, birds, insects and fish.

Published by Scholastic Inc.
90 Old Sherman Turnpike, Danbury, Connecticut 06816.

SCHOLASTIC and associated logos are trademarks of Scholastic Inc.

ISBN 0-7172-6689-3   Printed in the U.S.A.

Have you ever wondered . . .

Everyone is fascinated by leopards. Their mixture of strength and beauty is so striking that they have inspired countless folk tales. They have also been used by many organizations as a symbol for power and grace.

In West Africa about 200 years ago, people so admired the leopard's strength that even its whiskers were thought to have special powers. It was said that, chopped up and sprinkled in an enemy's food, they were sure to make the enemy sicken and die!

What is it about leopards that makes them both feared and admired? Let's take a closer look at these powerful, secretive animals.

Opposite page:
*A leopard surveys
its territory.*

Leopard Land

The leopard is the most widespread cat in the
world. That's partly because it isn't a picky
eater. A leopard will eat just about anything it
comes across, so it doesn't need to stick close to
any one type of animal or habitat.

Leopards are found in Africa, the Middle
East and southern Asia. They are equally at
home in tropical forests, open grasslands,
semideserts and even on mountainsides. They
can survive in very hot and very cold climates.
As long as there is water to drink and enough
cover so they can stalk their prey unseen,
leopards are happy.

*The colored areas
on this map show
where leopards
live.*

6

The Cat Family

The leopard is a member of the cat family. It has sharp claws, long whiskers and a fur coat just like a house cat. But the leopard can do something a house cat can't do—roar. The small cats, which include bobcats, lynx, cougars and house cats, cannot roar but they can purr. Lions, tigers, jaguars and leopards are known as big cats. They can roar, but they cannot purr—at least not continuously the way your pet cat can. Some of them can make purring sounds, but they have to stop to breathe.

Although there are several cats that are called leopards there is only one real leopard. The rare clouded leopard and the snow leopard, or ounce, are both distinct species from the leopard.

The snow leopard lives in the mountainous and forested regions of Asia.

9

Seeing Spots

The leopard's coat is spotted for a good reason. It makes it very difficult to see. Whether lying in long grass, in forest undergrowth or high up in a tree, its coat blends in perfectly with the patterns of light and shade around it. This helps make the leopard a good hunter. It can creep up very close to its prey without being seen.

A leopard is usually tawny yellow with blackish brown spots. On most of its body, the spots are arranged in rosettes. Rosettes are small circles made up of spots. The jaguar, the leopard's larger American cousin, has a very similar coat, but it is not quite the same. The difference is that the rosettes on a jaguar usually have one or more spots in the center, whereas those on the leopard hardly ever do.

The leopard has small spots on its head and larger ones on its body.

Spotless

There is one type of leopard that doesn't appear to have any spots at all. This leopard is sometimes called a ''black panther'' because its coat is so dark. But it isn't really black, it's a very dark shade of brown. And it does have spots. They are almost the same color as its background fur, however, and can only be seen when the animal is in bright sunlight.

The dark leopard is mainly found in moist, dense forests in Asia. It is quite rare. Although dark and tawny cubs may be born in the same litter, both parents must be dark in order to produce all dark cubs.

Can you spot the spots on this dark leopard's coat?

Mighty Cat

The leopard is the smallest member of the big cat family but it is very strong. A leopard weighs between 30 and 90 kilograms (66 to 198 pounds). That's less than half the size of a tiger. But a leopard has such powerful legs and jaws that it can carry its prey up into trees. That's pretty remarkable when the prey is a young zebra or antelope—animals that weigh at least as much as the leopard itself!

Leopards range in size from just under a metre to almost 2 metres (3 to 7 feet) in length. And that doesn't include their tail. Males are usually twice the size of females.

The leopard is an agile and graceful climber.

Tale of a Tail

A leopard's tail is thick and long—almost as long as its body, in fact. And it is very useful.

A mother leopard strokes her cubs with her tail. She also encourages them to play by waving it in front of them. When she tires of the game, she springs high up into a tree where the cubs cannot reach her. Her tail comes in handy there, too. It helps her to balance on branches with the ease of a tightrope walker.

The underside of a leopard's tail is usually white. As a mother leopard moves ahead of her young through thick undergrowth, she loops her tail up over her back, where it is easy for the cubs to see and follow.

A leopard's tail may grow to be a metre (3 feet) long.

Not Just a Cuddly Cat

Like the other big cats the leopard has long sharp claws. These come in handy for climbing trees and for hunting. When running the leopard retracts, or pulls its claws into its paws, to keep them sharp. This also helps it to approach its prey silently. When it is ready to spring the leopard extends its claws.

Along with its claws the leopard's long, pointed canine teeth help it to hold and kill its prey. The back teeth cut up the leopard's food into bite-sized pieces so it can be swallowed. And its rough tongue, which is covered in tiny hooks, is perfect for cleaning the last bits of meat off bones.

The soft pads on its feet and the fur between its toes help the leopard to walk quietly.

Leaping Leopards

The leopard is one of the super athletes of the animal kingdom. Although it usually moves slowly and silently, it can run up to 60 kilometres (40 miles) per hour when it needs to. That's faster than a car driving down a city street! No wonder the leopard can run at its top speed only in short spurts.

Leopards are also champion broad jumpers, able to cover more than 6 metres (20 feet) in a single bound. Even more amazingly, they can leap half that far straight up in the air. That's as high as a basketball hoop! And not only is the leopard the best tree climber in the big cat family, it is also a strong swimmer.

Keeping watch.

Leopard Language

Although leopards are not noisy animals, they can roar, grunt and make purring sounds. Their roar is more like a rasping cough than a mighty bellow, and the leopard uses it to contact other leopards, mostly at mating time. A male will also roar to let other males know they've entered his territory.

Zoologists observing leopards in the wild have noted at least two other leopard sounds: chuffling and chirping. Chuffling is a sound made by blowing air sharply through the nostrils. One zoologist heard a mother leopard chuffle to call her cubs. Another heard a leopard make an odd, high-pitched chirping noise whenever she was afraid for her cubs' safety.

Panting helps the leopard to cool off on a hot day.

Body Language

On the back of each of its rounded ears, the leopard has a white spot set against a black background. These spots, as well as the white underside of the leopard's tail, help cubs keep track of their mother when they are following her through thick underbrush. But why do males have them too when they hardly ever help care for the cubs? Some zoologists think that when leopards meet to mate, and on those rare occasions when they hunt together, they flick their ears a certain way to send messages. ''Come on over,'' ''Go away,'' or ''This way to the food!'' may all be signaled by ear movements.

Notice the white spot on the back of this leopard's ear.

Hide and Seek

Even now, we know more about lions, tigers and jaguars than we do about leopards. This is because leopards are very secretive. They are active mainly at night and their senses are specially suited for getting around in the dark.

In daylight, leopards probably see no better than you do, but a special reflective material in their eyes gives them excellent night vision. Their long whiskers help them at night too, by acting as feelers that warn them of branches and anything else in their path. Leopards also have a keen sense of smell and cup-shaped ears that move to pinpoint exactly where a sound is coming from. With their sensitive nose and exceptional hearing they can easily avoid people and can locate prey even if they can't see it. This is particularly useful when traveling through forests and dense vegetation.

Leopards almost always hunt alone.

Food, Glorious Food

The leopard is a carnivore, or meat eater. It feeds on just about anything that moves—from tiny beetles to young giraffes. Although a leopard mainly eats impala, other gazelles and wildebeest it will also dine on frogs, lizards, birds, monkeys, rats, pigs and baboons. It may supplement its meaty diet with grass, eggs and fruit.

Leopards have a taste for fish as well. They sometimes lie on the banks of rivers or lakes, flipping large fish out of the water with their paws.

A young leopard practices its stalking skills on a lizard.

Hunting Habits

Leopards usually hunt at night. Often they stalk their prey silently, slinking along with their belly close to the ground, before dashing forward and pouncing. Unsuspecting smaller prey are sometimes killed when they are resting without any chase at all. A leopard may also drop down from a tree branch onto prey passing below. It can hunt while in a tree, too, giving chase to the monkeys and birds that live there.

A leopard strangles its prey by grabbing it by the throat, or kills it with a bite to the back of the neck. Then it carries its prey high into the branches of a tree, beyond the reach of other meat-eaters, such as lions and wild dogs. If the animal is too large to eat all at once, the leopard will come back to feed day after day until there is nothing left. It doesn't care if the meat is rotten.

Pity the poor animal that comes strolling under this tree!

Private Property

Leopards live and hunt within an area known as their home range. The size of the range varies. Ten square kilometres (4 square miles) is plenty if there's lots of food and water. If either is in short supply, 40 square kilometres (16 square miles) might not be big enough.

Females often have overlapping ranges, but males refuse to share with each other. A male leopard warns other males off his territory by scratching trees and digging holes. He even sprays urine on trees to leave a scent that tells other males to keep out. If they're foolish enough not to take the hint, a fight will result. Luckily, the scents and signals are usually enough to send an unwanted visitor packing.

*Sometimes it's very tiring being
a leopard.*

Getting Together

For most of the year, leopards live alone. They even avoid each other's company. A male and female usually get together only to mate, then separate again after a few days. Though cases have been noted where the male helps raise the young by bringing food to them, this is far from common.

Mating takes place at any time of the year and cubs can be born in any season. The female attracts the male with a combination of smells and sounds. She travels far and wide, leaving scent markings for the male to follow or calling quietly with a special mating call. After mating she usually chases the male away.

The happy couple.

Cuddly Cubs

About three months after mating, the female leopard gives birth. She can have anywhere from one to six cubs, but usually has two or three.

The newborn leopards are quite small, weighing only about 450 grams (a pound), not much more than a young kitten. They are covered with dull gray fur that shows just a hint of spots, but their eyes are tightly shut and they are completely helpless.

It will be about a week or ten days before the cubs open glazed bluish eyes to get their first look at the world. Meanwhile they spend their time sleeping and nursing on their mother's rich milk.

You can tell that this cub is several weeks old by its clear blue eyes and its well-defined spots.

Early Days

The mother leopard hides her babies in a rock crevice or a hollow tree and usually transfers them to a new hiding place every few days. This makes it much harder for a hungry jackal, hyena or eagle to find them.

Mother and cubs enjoy being close to each other. The mother grooms her cubs often, and they greet each other by rubbing their faces or bodies together. When the cubs are a little older, they tumble and play fight at every opportunity.

You'd have to be very brave or very foolish—and probably both—to try to get near this mother's cub.

Growing Up

At first, the helpless cubs are guarded day and night by their mother. She leaves only when she has to hunt for food. While she is gone, the cubs never venture from the den, no matter how hungry they become.

When they are first allowed out under mother's watchful eye, they spend their time crouching motionless, camouflaged amongst the shadows. Soon, however, the cubs venture farther afield. They are the most vulnerable when they're not yet familiar with their surroundings. Small and weak, they are in danger of attack from predators. Fortunately their mother is devoted and tries to protect them from all intruders.

It's not long before a young leopard cub is following its mother everywhere.

Leopard Lessons

When they are four to six months old, the young cubs begin to accompany their mother on hunting trips. She teaches them how to hide from enemies and how to stalk and catch prey. These are not easy skills to acquire and the learning process can be dangerous. Sometimes prey will fight back, and a desperate baboon or wild pig may prove too much for a young cub to handle. Cubs are often hurt and sometimes killed. It could take almost two years before they are ready to hunt on their own.

All senses alert.

Leaving Home

The leopard cubs stay close to their mother until they are at least a year old. After that, they start to spend time on their own, gradually becoming more and more independent. By the time they are about two, the mother is ready to give birth to a new litter, and the youngsters must leave and fend for themselves.

The males set out to establish their own territory. Females usually take over part of their mother's range, though they rarely spend time with her. If they have learned their lessons well, the young leopards can expect to live about ten more years and have several families of their own.

Words to Know

Camouflage   Colors and patterns that help an animal blend in with its surroundings.

Canine tooth   One of four strong pointed teeth, located between the front teeth and the molars.

Carnivore   Literally, "meat eater." A mammal that feeds mainly on flesh.

Chuffling   A sound made by blowing air sharply through the nostrils.

Cub   A young leopard.

Habitat   The area or type of area in which an animal or plant naturally lives.

Home range   Area where an animal lives and hunts.

Predator   An animal that hunts other animals for food.

Prey   An animal hunted or killed by another animal for food.

Retract   Draw back into the body.

Rosette   A small circle made up of spots.

Territory   Area that an animal or group of animals lives in and often defends from other animals of the same kind.

Wildebeest   Large African antelope, also called gnu.

Zoologist   Scientist who studies animals.

INDEX

Cover Photo: Bill Ivy

Photo Credits: Bill Ivy, pages 4, 8, 12, 16-17, 21, 25, 26, 34; Peter Arnold/Hot Shots, page 7; Cynthia and Amor Klotzbach, page 11; G.C. Kelley, pages 15, 18; Superstock/Four By Five, pages 22, 33; Len Rue Jr., page 29; Breck Kent, pages 30, 38; Selwyn Powers (Sandved & Coleman), pages 37, 42; Len Lee Rue III, page 41; Kjell B. Sandved (Sandved & Coleman), page 45.

Getting To Know...

Nature's Children

PARROTS

Merebeth Switzer

SCHOLASTIC INC.

New York Toronto London Auckland Sydney
Mexico City New Delhi Hong Kong Buenos Aires

Facts in Brief

Classification of parrots

    Class: *Aves* (birds)

    Order: *Psittaciformes* (Parrot-like bird)

    Family: *Psitacidae* (Parrots, cockatoos, macaws and lories)

    Genus and Species: There are over three hundred kinds of parrots.

World distribution. Parrots are found in all tropical regions of the world.

Habitat. Tropical forests.

Distinctive physical characteristics. Usually very brightly colored; feet adapted for climbing and beak that is curved so that the bottom fits into the top.

Habits. Noisy and long-lived, parrots usually live in large groups. Many are good mimics and can repeat words and other sounds.

Diet. Mainly fruit and seeds.

Published by Scholastic Inc.
90 Old Sherman Turnpike, Danbury, Connecticut 06816.

SCHOLASTIC and associated logos are trademarks of Scholastic Inc.

ISBN 0-7172-6689-3   Printed in the U.S.A.

Have you ever wondered . . .

It is dawn and the jungle is just beginning to stir. Suddenly a loud, raspy screech pierces the air. Another screech, then another. The parrots are awake. They sit on their branches preening and calling, their bright colors glittering through the thick canopy of green leaves. Suddenly they swoop off to look for food. A new day has begun in the tropical forest.

Parrots have been known and loved by people for centuries. Ancient Roman emperors imported them from Africa and the Far East as pets and they have been popular ever since. Why? Most parrot lovers say it is because they are beautifully colored, curious and intelligent, and some can even mimic human speech. Let's take a closer look at these remarkable birds and see what their life is like in the wild.

The brilliantly colored crimson rosella makes its home in Australia.

A Big Family

The parrot family is one of the largest bird families in the world. There are more than 300 different kinds of parrots. The smallest are the tiny pygmy parrots of New Guinea, which are no bigger than the palm of your hand. The largest are the huge, colorful macaws that live in the Amazon. They are as tall as a four-year-old child!

Parrots and parakeets are the most obvious members of the parrot family. But did you know that budgies, cockatoos, cockatiels, lories, lorikeets and lovebirds are also part of the parrot clan?

The peach-faced lovebird is the largest member of its family. Lovebirds get their name from their habit of preening each other.

8

A Place Called Home

Most parrots live high up in the giant trees of the tropical rain forests of the world. However, a few unique parrots that can no longer fly live on the ground. In Australia, some parrots, like cockatoos and budgies, are also found in brush and grassland areas.

Parrots are found mainly on the continents of South America, Africa, Asia and Australia and on the islands in the Pacific Ocean. Some, like the Andean parakeet, can even survive in cool mountain air.

Top: At rest, the sulfur-crested cockatoo keeps its crest close to its head.
Bottom: This is what happens when a cockatoo is alarmed.

A Cracker of a Beak

You can recognize a parrot by its short, chunky, hooked beak. This beak is specially designed for cracking open the nuts and seeds parrots like to eat. The sharp pointed tip of the upper beak also comes in handy for digging into the bark of trees to haul out grubs.

A parrot's powerful beak is useful for more than just finding a meal. Those that live in dense forests sometimes use their beak to grasp branches and vines as they push themselves through the heavy vegetation. Also, a parrot can recover its balance by grabbing a nearby branch with its beak.

Like your fingernails, a parrot's beak is made of hard material that can wear down with use. This is not a problem for the parrot, because the beak keeps growing throughout the bird's life. In fact, if a parrot doesn't eat enough of the hard, crunchy foods that wear down the beak, the bird will have to rub it against a tree trunk or a rock to file it down.

Opposite page:
Macaws exercise their powerful beak by chewing anything within reach.

Family Resemblance

No matter how big a parrot is, its body looks very much like the bodies of all other parrots. Its large, rounded head is joined to its chunky body by a very short neck. The body then tapers from the shoulders, which gives the bird a shape like an upside-down egg.

Because they are mostly strong flyers, parrots have big chest muscles. That is why, when they are sitting, they look like they are wearing a football player's shoulder-pads!

A parrot's feet are very useful for life in the jungle. Why? With two toes facing frontward and two facing backward, the bird can easily climb up and down trees.

Red-crowned parrot.

Fine Feathers . . .

Like all birds, parrots lay eggs and have feathers covering their bodies. There are different kinds of feathers and they serve different purposes.

Very tiny, fluffy, *down* feathers help to insulate the parrot's body, keeping it from getting too cold at night or too hot when the tropical sun beats down during the day. Special *powder down* feathers, which keep growing throughout the bird's life, break off at the tip and crumble into a fine powder. Scientists think this powder helps to keep the parrot from getting soaked and catching a chill during a jungle rainstorm.

The red feathers of this Electus parrot identify it as a female. Males are primarily green.

And Feathers for Flying

Parrots also have *contour* feathers that give their body a streamlined shape for flying. And, of course, their stiff, strong wing feathers give them the ability to fly.

Some parrots—lories and cockatoos, for instance—have short, stubby tails. Others, such as macaws and parakeets, have very long tail feathers. Many of these parrots are extremely powerful fliers. They use their tails for balance and as a rudder to direct them through the air. And some of the long-tailed birds spread out their tail feathers like mini-parachutes to slow them down when they are landing.

The rainbow lorikeet is noisy as it flies from tree to tree, searching for food.

A Rainbow of Colors

Parrots have some of the most beautiful feathers in the animal world. Probably the dullest colored parrot is the African Gray parrot, but even this grayish-white bird has a red rump! The Amazon Green parrots are all different shades of brilliant green, with patches of yellow, red or orange for accent. Some parrots look as though they have had parts of their body dipped in paint. They may be bright pink, electric blue, metallic green or vibrant yellow. Some have all four colors splashed on different parts of their body.

Coat of many colors. (Solitary lory)

Why So Flashy?

In nature, many animals survive by being dull in color to blend in with the world around them. Not the parrot family! In fact, being brilliantly colored helps these birds to survive. How?

Parrots live in jungles where sunlight pokes through the trees and dapples the leaves. The foliage is bright green, and the flowers and fruits are often large and brightly colored. When a parrot sits in a tree in the forest, falcons, hawks and eagles—its most worrisome enemies—may well mistake it for an exotic bloom or a ripe fruit.

The gaudy coloring helps solve another problem parrots sometimes face: finding each other in the dark, thick green jungle. This is especially important if they are looking for a mate. Their brightly colored feathers help. And because both the male and female birds have the same coloring, they can recognize another of their own kind easily.

Opposite page: *Despite its vivid colors, the eastern rosella does blend in with its surroundings.*

Born Mimics

Generally, parrots don't really understand what they are saying, but some of them are great imitators and can copy any sound they hear regularly. This includes the sound of a tomcat howling, a door squeaking or a baby crying. Parrots that have lived with humans since they were very young have sometimes been taught to say many words and even quite long sentences. And because some parrots can live for more than a hundred years in captivity, they have plenty of time to learn new words!

The African Gray parrot is the most skilled mimic of all parrots.

Loud Mouth

While some parrots are noted for their ability to imitate the human voice, others are better known for their very loud, raucous squawks. In fact, people who thought that a parrot would make a good pet have discovered that most of them are noisy and have unpleasant screeching voices. There is a good reason for this. In the jungle, such a loud, unique call helps a parrot to recognize one of its own kind. Also, since a parrot's call can carry for great distances, it helps the birds keep in touch with each other.

The birds with the loudest, most objectionable voices are usually those like the macaws that live in pairs or small groups in the dense jungle. If the closest bird of a parrot's own species is the equivalent of two city blocks away, with a thick screen of vines, trees and flowers in between, a good loud call helps them to find each other.

The blue and yellow macaw is not only loud but is also a good talker.

Sharp Eyes and Ears

With such flashy colors and loud voices it seems obvious that most parrots have keen eyesight and good hearing. This is usually true—in fact, scientists believe that parrots are able to distinguish colors. If parrots saw only in black and white, they would have trouble telling a piece of ripe fruit from leaves or unripe fruit, and they wouldn't be able to identify another of their kind at a distance.

Hearing is also important to parrots, since the thick jungle growth often obscures their view of things. Parrots don't have big, floppy ears. Instead, they have ear openings tucked in under the feathers on the sides of their head. These openings may be small, but they are all a parrot needs to hear perfectly.

Even the eye of the amboina king parrot is beautiful.

On the Menu

Most parrots feed on plants, eating seeds, nuts, fruits, berries, leaves and even fresh green shoots. Seeds and nuts are especially important to some parrots. They use their beak and their big fleshy tongue to get at the food inside.

Have you ever tried to open Brazil nuts without using a nutcracker? Well, just imagine how strong a macaw's beak must be. It can crack open Brazil nuts as easily as you can break a peanut shell.

Scarlet macaw.

A Dinner of Nectar or Worms

The brilliantly colored lories and lorikeets found in New Guinea, Indonesia and Australasia feed on nectar, pollen and fruit. Their beaks are more slender than those of most parrots, and their tongue has a special brush-like tip. They crush the flower blossoms with their beaks and then lap up the drops of nectar.

There are a few parrots that have developed a taste for meat. These birds prefer a dinner of slugs, larvae and wood-boring worms. And cockatoos dig into the ground to find root vegetables similar to potatoes to eat.

The rainbow lorikeet feeds not only on nectar but also on fruit, pollen, berries and insects.

Daily Routine

Most parrots are quite sociable. They spend much of their time together in a flock following the same daily routine. They awaken before sunrise and begin a noisy chorus of calls and screeches. All this noise helps to bond the flock together. It lets each parrot know where the others are, even if it can't see them through the dense vegetation.

After preening their feathers and grooming themselves, the birds move off in search of a good feeding area. There they eat until they are full. Sometimes they may move on to new areas to find more food. Near midday they descend to the cool pools of the forest floor for a drink and a refreshing splash. This is the hottest part of the day, so the parrots pick shady places to rest and relax.

As the cooler evening hours approach, the flock rouses itself and heads off for an evening meal and drink. When darkness sets in, and after a few squabbles over perches, they settle into their treetop roosts and sleep.

Opposite page:
Tidying up!

35

Finding a Mate

Although many parrots flock together, when nesting time comes most of them pair up to look for a suitable nest. Most parrots mate when they develop their adult feathers at two to four years of age. Some of the larger kinds, however, are not ready to have a family of their own until they are eight to ten years old.

Many types of parrots, including macaws and most Amazon parrots, spend their entire life with one mate. Only if one of the pair dies will the other seek a new mate.

Parrots have different ways of showing their interest in each other. Those that have mated for life roost with their bodies pressed tightly against each other. They also groom each other, and sometimes they kiss and rub each other's necks affectionately.

Birds of a feather stay together.

Parrot Apartments

Almost all parrots nest in holes—in trees, in the ground or among rocks and tree roots. They either take over existing holes, possibly making a few alterations, or they use their strong beaks to hollow out a new hole. Some kinds of parrots even hollow out burrows in termite nests!

Parrot nests don't usually appear to be very comfortable. Unlike many other birds that line their nests with grass and feathers, most parrots lay their eggs right on the scratchy wood chips or whatever else happens to be lying in the hollow they scrape for their eggs.

Like penguins, some parrots nest together in large groups called colonies. For example, the Monk parakeets of South America build their own "apartment buildings." Each pair of birds builds a nest, which they join to other nests with twigs and vines. When the gigantic common nest is completed, each family has its own "apartment."

Macaws nest in holes often well above the ground.

Laying Eggs

After the parrots have built their nest, the female begins to lay eggs. Depending on the species, she will lay one to ten pure white eggs, usually one egg every other day. It may take up to two weeks before all her eggs are laid.

Parrots' nests are usually well hidden from the eyes of hungry predators. The eggs are white because they have no need of protective coloring.

The male parrot stays with the female, usually fetching food for her while she sits on the eggs. However, some types of parrots, such as cockatoos, share the egg-sitting duties.

A pair of very rare gang-gang cockatoos.

The Babies Are Born

The eggs hatch about three weeks after they are laid. For some parrots this creates a rather unusual family situation because it means the chicks may be up to two weeks apart in age. With these fast-growing babies, that can make quite a difference!

Newly hatched chicks are not terribly appealing. They are naked, helpless and blind. Fortunately the chicks develop quickly. Within a few days they can see out of their big, bulging eyes and their little bodies are covered in fluffy gray or white down.

The chicks remain in the nest for anywhere from one to three months, and both parents are kept busy feeding them during this time. When the young ones are ready to venture out of the nest, they have a full set of feathers just like their parents and are equipped to fly.

Parrot chicks, like other baby birds, find their first flight tricky. But they are strong and can soon keep up with their parents.

Opposite page:
These Pesquet's parrot chicks will grow up to be large and bulky with a small hawk-like head.

Growing Up

Even though the young can get around, the parents continue to feed them. For some it may be several more months before they are fully on their own. The parrot chicks use this time to learn about the world around them. Games of chase through the dense jungle help them to master their flying skills. Mock battles to determine who will be the "king of the tree branch" help them learn how to defend their home turf and keep their balance under pressure.

For parrots, growing up is a time to play and a time to become strong so they can survive to raise a family of their own.

Yellow-crowned parrot.

Parrots and People

For generations and in almost all cultures, people have kept parrots as pets. But as their wilderness homes disappear, parrots are becoming rare throughout the world. Most countries now agree that the members of the parrot family, with the exception of a few domestic birds such as budgies, need our protection. It is now illegal in most countries to own or import parrots of any kind for pets. This includes most parrots, macaws and cockatoos. As well, efforts are being made to help preserve the tropical jungles that parrots call home. Many people now realize that these birds are very precious and that it is important to help them survive.

Words To Know

Colony   A large group of parrot pairs nesting in the same area.

Contour feathers   Feathers that help streamline a bird to let it fly through the air more smoothly.

Down   Very soft fluffy feathers.

Flock   A large group of birds.

Hatch   To break out of an egg.

Mate   To come together to produce young. Either member of an animal pair is also the other's mate.

Nectar   The sweet liquid produced by plants.

Plumage   A bird's feathers.

Powder down   Feathers that crumble into fine powder that helps to waterproof the parrot's other feathers.

Preening   Cleaning and oiling the feathers.

INDEX

Cover Photo: Columbus Zoo

Photo Credits: John Cancalosi, pages 4, 15, 16; E.R. Degginger, pages 7, 12, 20; Bill Ivy, pages 8, 35; Cincinnati Zoo, page 11; Zoological Society of San Diego, pages 19, 25, 41; A. Sandrin (Focus Stock Photo), pages 22, 23; Columbus Zoo, pages 27, 31; Kjell Sandved, page 28; Tourism Australia, page 33; Academy of Natural Sciences, pages 36, 39; Ron Garrison (Zoological Society of San Diego), page 43; Y. Arthus-Bertrand (Peter Arnold Inc./Hot Shots), page 45.